A REFLECTION
OF MY JOURNEY

A REFLECTION
OF MY JOURNEY

A LIFE EXPERIENCE THAT
HIGHLIGHTS GLOBAL ISSUES

DESMOND TOMLINSON

MANGIFERA
BLOOM

Port St Lucie

Copyright © 2021 Desmond Tomlinson
All rights reserved.

Published by Mangifera Bloom, Port St Lucie

All rights reserved. No part of this book may be reproduced, stored, or transmitted by any means—whether auditory, graphic, mechanical, or electronic—without written permission of the publisher except in the case of brief excerpts used in critical articles and reviews.
Please send inquiries to mangiferabloom@gmail.com.

Find out more at https://www.fosteringthroughtheeyesofachild.net

1st Edition

ISBN: 978-1-7342500-8-4 (Paperback)
ISBN: 978-1-7342500-9-1 (ebook)

Library of Congress Control Number: 2020923820

Edited by Mikel Benton
Cover illustration by Michael Rohani
Book design by DesignForBooks.com

Printed in the U.S.A.

CONTENTS

OVERVIEW   VII

   Life with my Father   vii
   Life at the Orphanage   ix
   Life with my Mother   x
   Foster Parent Experience   x

CHAPTER 1   THE STARTLING REVELATION   1

   A Deeper Meaning   1
   The Undeniable Truth   2
   Exploitation through Coercion and Deception   4
   Unorthodox Philosophies   5
   Hypocrisy and Exceptionalism   11
   The Insanity Complex   13
   Accountability   20

CHAPTER 2   MY BELIEFS AND PHILOSOPHY   27

CONCLUSION: WHAT HAVE WE LEARNED?   33

REFERENCES   35

OVERVIEW

In writing my history, I uncovered that one person's story can highlight issues socially and globally. The behavior that occurs on a personal level translates to the behavior exhibited by cultures, societies, and nations. After many years of praying and examining the evidence being presented, I have come to believe that there is a profound correlation between how people behaved towards me as a child and how people generally behave in society, both good and bad. To fully understand this revelation, I recommend that you first read the four volumes that constitute my autobiography. After you are through, I hope that you can take some time and reflect on what has been revealed concerning the past, present, and future. I also hope you can take some time and reflect on your own life experiences similarly. With that said, I would like to commence writing my reflection by providing you with a brief overview of my life's journey.

LIFE WITH MY FATHER

The first twenty-three years of my life's journey transpired on the island of Jamaica. Throughout the first seven years of my childhood, I lived in the parish of Westmoreland with my father, Clement Tomlinson, and my three older siblings, Pauline, Paulette, and George Tomlinson.

Throughout such time, I had no recollection that my family structure was missing the most important family member, my mother.

While living with our father, my siblings and I were subjected to a strict form of the Rastafarian doctrine. We were brought up in this manner because our father embraced the Rastafarian philosophy passionately. The Rastafarian doctrine was deeply rooted in our lives, as I outlined in volume 1 of my autobiography.

Throughout such time, my understanding was limited concerning the Rastafarian philosophy. However, as I continued to document my life's story, I found myself searching for answers to why my father had chosen to embrace this lifestyle. In my quest for deeper understanding, I discovered that the Rastafarian doctrine came into being as an alternative to the one being imposed on the black race by their oppressors, mainly "Great" Britain. This was a way for the black race to reconnect to their African roots and their ancestors from the Mother Land, Africa.

During the initial stage of compiling my autobiography, I was critical of my father's actions concerning his children. I was distraught with him for isolating us from the perceived norms of society. I was upset with him for not allowing us to attend school and for allowing us to consume marijuana. I hold my father accountable for the many unintended consequences his actions caused, most notably the many upheavals his children endured. I blamed my father for the inhumane treatment and outright abuse that my brother and I suffered at our foster parents' hands.

Throughout my quest for answers, I came to realize that my father had good intentions when he removed his children from what he described as the oppressive

Babylonian system. This deeper understanding also led me to believe that my father viewed Rastafarianism as a noble alternative to the system that has enslaved an entire race of people, the black race. Therefore, to address inequalities and regain the black race's identity, my father embraced the Rastafarian philosophy. However, his way of life triggered many unintended physical and psychological consequences. He was physically abused (Beaten severely with machetes by the police, which resulted in bodily harm, many years of physical and mental suffering, and eventually his untimely death), arrested, had his marijuana plantation destroyed, and finally, his children were removed from his care by the authorities.

LIFE AT THE ORPHANAGE

For the next two years, I found myself being torn physically, mentally, and emotionally between the Rastafarian doctrine and societal norms, as depicted by the orphanage. Shortly after my seventh birthday, this saga commenced when the authorities removed my siblings and me from our father's care. My sisters were eventually returned to our father's care after being turned away by the orphanages simply because they were Rastafarians. While at the orphanage, my brother and I were subjected to radical transformations, which included fundamental changes in our communication, diet, and religious practices. We were not allowed to communicate using the Rastafarian dialect, forced to consume meat and salt, and forced to conform to Christianity.

After several months of harsh and painful transformation, we were reunited with our father and sisters and reintroduced to the Rastafarian doctrine, including daily marijuana smoking, meditation, and chants. After approximately a year, the authorities raided our home once more, took us away from our father's care, and transferred us to different orphanages. My brother and I were returned to the Garland Hall Children's home, while my sisters were transferred to another orphanage. Once again, my brother and I were forced to conform to societal norms. After approximately two years of back and forth between our father's care and the orphanage, George and I were then transferred to our mother's care.

LIFE WITH MY MOTHER

This was the first time that I could remember witnessing my mother. Due to extreme poverty, our lives were all about survival, which had little or nothing to do with societal norms, including school, Christianity, or Rastafarianism. After approximately a year of living with our mother, the authorities removed us from her care and returned us to the orphanage (Garland Hall Children's Home). This was the case because our basic social and biological needs were not being met. Once again, we had no other choice but to conform to societal norms as depicted by the orphanage.

FOSTER PARENT EXPERIENCE

After living at the orphanage for several months, the authorities transferred my brother and me to a foster home where we had to conform to new norms. Unfortunately, our foster parents treated us as though our lives were insignificant and had no value, except to enrich them. They even used Christianity as a tool to control rather than a form of solemn worship. After enduring a little over three and a half years of physical and psychological abuse, my brother ran away from home. He was later transferred to a juvenile detention center by the very foster parents who had been entrusted to provide him a better life. This they did only because he spoke out against their injustice. This was an emotional separation that is very painful to explain with words. After five years of constant physical and psychological abuse, I also decided to confront my foster parents regarding their injustice. Instead of acknowledging their wrongs and changing their ways, they removed me from their care and returned me to the Child Development Agency. That day truly felt as though all hope had been lost and that my life had no value.

However, my hope was restored when I was provided with a temporary foster home and later a wonderful foster parent, Aunt Lucy, who intervened and supported me in every way possible. She removed my fears and elevated my hopes and dreams, and made me realize that I am a person and that my life should be valued. She gave me the courage and determination to persevere against all the odds. Her love and overwhelming compassion opened my eyes and my understanding to realize the true meaning of fostering. The details of this episode have been documented in volumes 2 and 3 of my autobiography.

CHAPTER 1

THE STARTLING REVELATION

This chapter is exclusively about a revelation that brought to light the profound correlation between my former foster parents' actions and ours today. This parallel has revealed the undeniable truth concerning our future and the urgent need for us to cease the actions that are deemed harmful to humanity. To put this chapter in context, please read volume 2 of my autobiography.

A DEEPER MEANING

As I set out to document my story, my hope was to have us examine ourselves and think deeply about the consequences of our actions, especially the type of behavior exemplified by my former foster parents. However, God has opened my eyes to an even bigger picture and made me realize that my former foster parents'

- utter disregard for the well-being of the children,
- profound exceptionalism,
- self-righteous attitudes,

Chapter 1

- blatant hypocrisy,
- unsatisfied monetary greed,
- unending quest to acquire and stockpile many beating devices, and
- the need to inflict physical and psychological harm to the innocent children

are, without a doubt, a microcosm of what is being exhibited today by cultures, societies, and nations.

Highlighting the profound correlation between my former foster parents' actions and those exhibited by us today was certainly not an easy undertaking. I also realized that this was precisely the path my brother had chosen when he decided to confront our foster parents concerning their injustice. Unfortunately, he was unable to change their hearts and minds in such regard. Not only was he unsuccessful in his quest, but those he pleaded with stripped him of his human dignity, and eventually his life. Given that my brother had been unsuccessful in changing two peoples' hearts and minds, I found myself pondering whether my effort to ask the world to cease the actions deemed harmful to humanity might end up becoming a futile undertaking. Nonetheless, I believe that my brother's message must be echoed to the world, irrespective of the costs.

THE UNDENIABLE TRUTH

For many years, I have searched for answers concerning the abuse suffered by my father at the hands of the authorities and later, the abuse suffered by the foster children, including my brother, but was unable to find any justification other than we were merely unfortunate people. However, after writing my memoir, I realized that concerning God, nothing happens by chance, no such thing as an unfortunate situation, and most certainly, there are no coincidence or mistake. Before this convincing truth, I regarded myself as a victim of the world's injustice rather than a contributor to the world's problems. I thought that I had nothing to do with the vicious cycle of atrocities and deceitful actions being perpetrated throughout the world today. However, after careful examination and deep soul searching, I came to the realization that *I am/we are* just as guilty as my former foster parents and even the many mass murderers whose hearts and minds could not be persuaded. Although it took me a while to accept this premise, I finally had to do so when a little voice whispered in my ears, "Thin veils and imaginary lines are what we have erected and have drawn between our harmful actions and those being harmed." Therefore, today, I am no longer ignorant of the obvious truth.

I also realized that my former foster parents' fate is a solemn reminder that the superficial things, including our mortal bodies that we cherish dearly, cannot and will not outlast their appointed time. Everything in this life has an expiration date. As noted in the scripture, we brought nothing when we came into this world, and we cannot take anything with us when we leave this world. Therefore, we should not bind our moral fiber with actions that result in ill-gotten financial or material gains, especially those that set out to harm children. My former foster parents' actions are best summed up in first Timothy 6:9 (ESV): "But those who desire to be rich fall into temptation, into a snare, into many senseless and harmful desires that plunge people into ruin and destruction." Their senseless and harmful desires plunged my brother's life into ruin and, eventually, an untimely death.

EXPLOITATION THROUGH COERCION AND DECEPTION

My former foster parents' injustice went unchallenged, which in turn prolonged the suffering of the children. They used their superficial religious status and economic wealth to influence the majority, including the church and the Child Development Agency. Whenever my brother, George, spoke out against their injustice, they denied him his meals and other basic necessities until he was forced to conform to their demands. They resorted to extreme and coercive measures to send a clear message that no one should dare challenge their authority. Although George was the one who toiled day after day to take care of the chickens and livestock, his hard work was overlooked and, at times, discredited. They indulged in illicit child-labor practices to enhance their wealth and prestige while ignoring the children's well-being. Putting one's selfish interest above human dignity is mostly how the systems of the world operate.

It was heartrending for me to witness my brother enduring hunger day after day while our foster parents had an abundance of food. A practice such as this is inhumane and should be considered a crime against humanity, especially when it is used to silence the voices that cry out for justice. The practice of withholding the basic life-sustaining essentials from a person or an entire nation just to have one's way is an immoral act that should not be supported and should not be tolerated! This is even more pressing in situations in which innocent children are being harmed!

Based on this experience, I would like to say that if a person, a system, or a nation's riches are attained through coercive measures, through the afflictions they impose on others, especially the innocent children, then such riches are insignificant and have no value. When our joy and happiness are attained through coercive measures, then we are displaying a facade, and our "joy and happiness" are nothing more than a charade. This is why I would like to say that it is immoral and inhumane to deprive or to withhold the basic life-sustaining essentials from the less fortunate. My earnest plea is for us to never again become the silent majority in situations where injustice abounds. As citizens of this world, we should rise up and challenge injustice in all its forms, whether they are perpetrated by a person, system, or nation.

UNORTHODOX PHILOSOPHIES

Religion should not be used as a means by which persons, systems, or nations enrich themselves or attain power and dominance. No persons, systems, or nations should think or act as though they are more righteous than others simply because they profess Christianity or adhere to a different form of religious, social, or economic philosophy. In fact, I would rather not be told or be reminded of what religious, social, or economic philosophy we profess, but instead that we be seen and judged by our deeds. It is ok to share with someone our faith or beliefs, but we must do so without using force or resorting to coercive behaviors and, at times, violent actions. The conviction of the heart is based on the exemplary lives we live and the God we serve.

Chapter 1

On the one hand, my former foster parents met all the requirements to be thought of as religious persons, while on the other hand, they lacked compassionate hearts.

The nineteenth-century abolitionist and statesman, Frederick Douglas, recounts an incident that is analogous to the conduct of my former foster parents. He writes:

> "In August, 1832, my master attended a Methodist camp-meeting held in the Bay-side, Talbot county, and there experienced religion. I indulged a faint hope that his conversion would lead him to emancipate his slaves, and that, if he did not do this, it would, at any rate, make him more kind and humane. I was disappointed in both these respects. It neither made him to be humane to his slaves, nor to emancipate them. If it had any effect on his character, it made him more cruel and hateful in all his ways; for I believe him to have been a much worse man after his conversion than before. Prior to his conversion, he relied upon his own depravity to shield and sustain him in his savage barbarity; but after his conversion, he found religious sanction and support for his slaveholding cruelty. He made the greatest pretensions to piety. His house was the house of prayer. He prayed morning, noon, and night. He very soon distinguished himself among his brethren, and was soon made a class-leader and exhorter. His activity in revivals was great, and he proved himself an instrument in the hands of the church in converting many souls. His house was the preachers' home. They used to

The Startling Revelation

take great pleasure in coming there to put up; for while he starved us, he stuffed them. We have had three or four preachers there at a time." (Douglas, p. 54–55).

I do not mean to say that the coerced servitude and degradation I experienced as a child was as severe as what Frederic Douglas knew in his time. My purpose is to draw attention to the contradiction between professed religious beliefs and conduct.

My relationship with God was never contingent upon my former foster parents' hypocritical religious personae. Their actions would provide most anyone with reasons to reject God and Christianity outright. Today, I am grateful that my beliefs and relationship with God stood apart from any particular form of religion or religious doctrines.

After a careful and deliberate thought process, I found myself asking several fundamental questions concerning religion. As I reflected on the time I spent at the orphanage, I began to ask myself why it was important for missionaries to travel from other parts of the world, mostly Europe and the United States of America, to bring religion to a child residing at an orphanage. Not only that, but I have also witnessed mentally challenged children being forced against their will to sit still and listen to the missionaries. As for me, I did not really understand much of what was being taught. From my perspective, any person or group of people that came to the orphanage was really there to feed us. As a matter of fact, I was really there hoping to receive a pack or two of the delicious, mouthwatering cookies they would provide us after they were through teaching. Nonetheless, the things that registered in my mind to this

Chapter 1

very day are the attributes of love and compassion that the missionaries taught us concerning Jesus and how we should strive to be like him. This religious teaching was not only taught at the orphanage, but it was also instilled in me by my former foster parents, as I outlined in volume 2 of my autobiography.

Despite the many years of indoctrination, both Rastafarianism and Christianity, today I realize that I have very few answers concerning the intricacies of life's religious and philosophical questions. However, as I become more aware of how Christianity is being practiced, I realize that our systems and leaders seldom embrace Jesus's traits, especially those that include love, compassion, impartiality, concern for justice, and the willingness to sacrifice for others. Instead, we have exempted our leaders and institutions from adhering to those fundamental principles. Shouldn't the missionaries, comrades, and leaders adhere to the principles that the orphanage children are taught? If we can go to great lengths to force orphan children who are mentally challenged to be like Jesus, then it causes me to wonder what excuse do we of sound minds have?

I have witnessed this separation or exemption mindset being exercised by my former foster parents. They knew how to separate the religious lives they portrayed at church and other public venues from the ones they portrayed at home. They viewed their religion to be very sacred, thus displaying zero tolerance in such regard. While, to the contrary, they neglected and, in many instances, undermined the very fabric of human dignity concerning the innocent children placed in their care. Unfortunately, these are not just my former foster parents' shortcomings; they are ours too.

The Startling Revelation

I also realize how easy it is for us to claim that we are God-fearing people and God-fearing nations, while our actions do not reflect the moral principles associated with those assertions. I often find myself asking what my father meant when he claimed that the systems of this world should not be trusted and that those who profess Christianity are hypocrites. In the same context, I also find myself wondering if the "I love you" phrase that we repeat so often is a solemn vow coming from our hearts or just another ritual that we evoke solely as a courtesy gesture.

Many of us who profess Christianity need to be reminded that the attributes of Jesus should not just be something we teach but something that we should emulate.

As a whole, the church should not sacrifice moral principles in its quest to acquire wealth by luring or retaining membership of those who seek to use their money or social status to fulfill or advance their own selfish desires. This is even more pressing when we know that such individuals are using ill-gotten gains to influence the church. Concerning Christianity, I believe that only Jesus Christ should influence the church!

This is why everyone should be mindful not to ignore the injustice committed before our eyes only because it is directed at someone else. If we do, then it will only be a matter of time before the injustice we ignore today becomes the injustice we face tomorrow when it is being directed at us. In this situation, I have to hold myself accountable because I did not side with my brother in his quest for justice. When he spoke against our foster parents' injustice, I advised him to not do so. When we were labeled dogs and scavengers, and my brother told our foster mother that it was wrong to address us in such a manner, I told him not to speak out because he was making life more difficult for the foster children. I opposed my brother because I was worried that we would lose the few life-sustaining necessities our foster parents provided us.

However, the day I spoke out against my foster parent's injustice was the very day I was no longer welcome at their home. That was the day I reaped the same fate my brother had. This is a reminder that when faced with injustice, we should not throw our hands up and say, "It is what it is, and there is nothing we can do about it."

Another misguided perception concerning religion is that we tend to convince ourselves and others that we are blessed when we are taking advantage of the less fortunate to amass wealth. Wealth amassed by exploiting others, whether the strong or the most vulnerable, should at no time be considered as a blessing from God. Ill-gotten gains should not be confused with God bestowing blessings upon a person, system, or nation! Therefore, we—as people, systems, and nations—need to be mindful so that we do not find ourselves ceding moral ground to others simply because of their economic, religious, or political influence. This was the case with many who knew precisely the abuse that my foster parents were guilty of but who failed to act. However, there are individuals such as Aunt Lucy, my neighbor Mrs. Lee, and my Child Development Agency representatives, Ms. Davis and Mrs. Stewart, who stood up for justice and pushed back against coercive behaviors. These individuals did not adhere to my former foster parents' fabricated lies. Instead, through a deliberate, thoughtful, and thorough process, they examined my former foster parents' accusations and questioned their motives.

Unfortunately, my brother never received the same justice. His accusers were not challenged. Neither were their motives uncovered. Therefore, when we have examined a matter, whether it be a simple accusation or an allegation that will result in a dire consequence, let us not conceal, deny, or walk away from our responsibilities because the truth does not align with our interests. Let us not be swayed by our own interests concerning how much we have to gain or how much we stand to lose. Instead, the truth should be our only guiding principle and not the allegiance we have concerning a person, system, or nation. This precept is even more crucial concerning those who set out to manipulate others through coercion and deception. Neither should we let the allegiance we have concerning our fellow humankind or inanimate things supersede the core principle that all human beings have the fundamental right to liberty and the freedom to pursue their destinies. In this regard, there should be no exception!

HYPOCRISY AND EXCEPTIONALISM

My former foster parents' self-proclaimed exceptionalism was the main reason why they were treated as though they were above reproach. They were able to influence many as a result of their economic, social, and religious status. They sanctioned disciplinary measures for others, including church members, who had committed lesser transgressions than they were guilty of committing, not to mention those concerning the innocent children. They used politics, religion, and even the very Bible to justify their wrongdoings. However, I realized that they were only using these things to achieve their selfish desires. When my brother would no longer be of any benefit to them, they labeled him an evil person and levied all sorts of baseless accusations against him with the intent to destroy his life.

Today, we can see the very same hypocrisies and acclaimed exceptionalism on display. We use economics, politics, religion, and even the Bible to get others to conform, while, to the contrary, the adherence we are demanding of others does not apply to us. We are quick to identify others' faults but not our own. We dismiss and, even at times, discredit those who dare to confront us concerning our harmful actions. We punish others for their wrongdoings while we use exceptionalism to justify our harmful actions. And in so doing, we have exempted ourselves and those aligned with our interests. In this context, I would ask, what premise do we as individuals, systems, and nations use to justify our actions? Do we invoke moral principles only when we need others to conform? Is our premise based on moral principles that are immune to our race, nationality, and economic interests? Or is it based on self-proclaimed exceptionalism, which stipulates that we are superior to the other? The hypocrisy demonstrated by my foster parents reminds us how easy it is for us to examine the characters of others while, at the same time, ignoring the fact that character examination should start from within.

It is quite difficult for me to understand; especially knowing that my former foster parents used Jesus as their guide when teaching about love, compassion, humility, peace, joy, and happiness, while their actions reflected the opposite. Were their teachings, preaching, praying, and worshipping not genuine? Shouldn't their lives have been a reflection of what they preached and what they taught? They have neglected and undermined the very fabric of human dignity concerning the innocent children in their care. These are not just my former foster parents' shortcomings; they are ours too. We claimed to be righteous, but unfortunately, our systems very seldom reflect the traits that we teach and preach.

I believe strongly that when a person, system, or nation proclaims exceptionalism and superiority over others, it becomes dangerous. History shows that people who assume superiority over others use this belief as a license for exploiting and harming others. In my view, superiority and exceptionalism are concepts that best belong to God alone! None is above reproach! My brother pleaded for justice, but unfortunately, the faint cry of the minority was simply not persuasive enough. The more that I reflect on this experience, the more I realize that my brother's cry for justice, although at the time directed toward our foster parents, is one that needs to be echoed throughout the entire world. And this time, I would hope that the faint cry of the minority would not go unnoticed.

THE INSANITY COMPLEX

The need to acquire and stockpile many beating devices to inflict physical and psychological harm to the children was one of my former foster parents' actions that is still quite difficult for me to come to terms with. The elaborate process they went through to acquire those enhanced leather straps and the time and effort exerted to cut and shape the many pieces of sticks and garden hoses into beating devices has caused me to wonder what was going on in their minds. It was certainly not a pleasant sight witnessing our foster mother preparing and stockpiling those punishment

Chapter 1

devices. The foster children were terrified to be in our foster parents' presence, more so our foster mother. I often found myself asking why my foster parents needed so many beating devices. Why would they exert so much effort to ensure that the next device they acquired has the potential to cause more harm than the one they already had? I believe that they indulged in these abusive behaviors to make sure that we conformed to their injustice.

At first, I could not correlate my former foster parents' need to stockpile many beating devices with any other actions that are taking place in the world today. However, after many years of pondering and praying, I realized that in this context, my foster parent's actions reflected the same kind of human failings that lead to the harmful instruments of war that are being amassed by nations. The leatherworker who was the creator and supplier of the potentially lethal leather straps is a prime example of those who manufacture and supply weapons of war with little or no regard for those being harmed in the process. This we do while knowing full well that weapons of war have no other purpose but to bring about intimidation, death, and destruction. In this context, our actions defy all logic and rational reasoning. We are stockpiling these weapons, knowing full well that they could be used by irresponsible parties to wage war against our fellow humankind.

I am quite confident that if a concerned person had asked my foster parents and the supplier of the leather straps to justify their actions, they would most certainly have provided a compelling rationale. Today, this very mindset is no different from how we justify the need to manufacture and supply weapons of war. Even when our actions embody the very essence of insanity, we continue to seek justification because the monetary value and the superficial status have become deeply entrenched in our lives.

Baseless accusations (evil, bad, rude, ill-mannered) were levied against the foster children, which became the pretext for our foster parents' acquisition and stockpiling of all those beating devices. The evidence revealed that the accusations were nothing more than a disguise our foster parents used to justify their abuse related to the children. They denigrated the truth my brother was conveying to the point where their lies started to come across as believable. Therefore, it is in this context that I am sincerely asking everyone to please examine the accusations or charges that a person, system, or nation has levied against another person, system, or nation. By doing so, we can establish the accuser's motives before we rush to judgment.

It is not uncommon for persons, systems, or nations to fabricate matters to justify their actions and the actions of those who seek to benefit from the outcomes. So let us exercise great patience while we thoroughly examine the accusers' accusations. And if we lack such a guiding principle, let us seek wise councils based on the moral principles that define how we should treat others. Therefore, let us not hinder or suppress our God-given ability to reason concerning the indisputable evidence that is made available to us. These are the essential measures that we need to employ so that we do not find ourselves becoming instruments of the accusers' deceptive behaviors and practices. This is even more essential in situations in which grave harm is brought to bear on innocent children. A thorough examination is also more pressing when the accuser has claimed to be morally superior to the accused. My former foster parents' claimed to be superior, which was why they labeled the foster children, more so my brother, as dogs and scavengers. It was the innocent children, including my only brother, who suffered immensely due to such a deceptive scheme.

The same question I asked concerning my former foster parents can also be asked of all nations who conceive, purchase, and trade war instruments. What is the rationale for so many destructive weapons when it takes only one to cause death and destruction to thousands, if not millions, of lives? Why is it that humanity is always on a quest to acquire more of the very things that have no other purpose than to destroy lives? What is the mental state of those who decide that weapons that have the potential to kill thousands are not adequate, so let them acquire others that have the potential to kill millions? Is this the perceived norm that we have come to accept? Are these the so-called morals and values that we uphold? Is this a reflection of what we deem to be our "sanity"?

I believe wholeheartedly that we are cognizant of our harmful past, because we are quick to remove portraits and other forms of emblematic references to Hitler and other mass murderers from among us. However, we are not so quick to do the same concerning the weapons of war used by these individuals to bring about fear, intimidation, death, and destruction. We are quite conscious of the evil and atrocities committed by the deceased while, to the contrary, we have ignored the same concerning the living. Not only that, but it is unequivocally clear that the living are the ones prolonging the vicious cycle of atrocities.

Today, we are spending much of our time and precious resources perfecting what those mass murderers started through the creation, dissemination, and use of such weapons. And if there was ever a time in history when humanity should have completely turned away from such practices, it was after witnessing the human toll caused by the atomic bomb. Instead, we have woven these destructive weapons into every aspect of our lives, thus making it all the more difficult for us to rid ourselves of them. This conduct embodies the highest order of insanity that we have allowed to become acceptable norms! After witnessing the devastating destruction that took place in our most recent past, only our egos are preventing us from implementing a cease and desist order concerning wars and the instruments of war.

Our egos have become malignant tumors that are suffocating our consciences. As a result, we can no longer see the danger that is fomenting before our eyes. It is irresponsible of us to think that both humans and weapons of war can coexist safely. We have overlooked and are continuing to ignore the fact that wars began the very day we have decided to manufacture and disseminate weapons of war.

Therefore, it is only a matter of time before we are consumed by our egos and resort to the use of such weapons, thereby causing irreparable harm to humanity as a whole. However, we tend to ignore this possibility because we see a "righteous" version of ourselves whenever we look in the mirror. We are marching down a destructive path based on our own accord, but when asked to change, we are pretending as though we need a greater force than our will to reverse course. With this mindset, we are undoubtedly teetering toward the brink of a disaster that will be of epic proportions!

Not only are we stockpiling weapons of war, but it is through this insane practice that we have assigned unto ourselves superficial titles and self-proclaimed glory, such as "superpower," of a world that we have not created, that we have not fully explored, and whose natural forces we are unable to control fully. Nothing indicates that humans are the masters of this world, much less the universe. In our recklessness, we ignore our limitations and the damage we are doing to the planet. It is becoming clear how arrogant we have become by assuming our superficial titles allow us to have ultimate control over the natural forces around us! Instead of being the wise custodians of God's creation, our egos have overtaken us. We seemed to have forgotten that humility teaches wisdom, but ego embodies and extends folly. We can choose to ignore the warnings and risk losing what we observe all around us, but we need to realize we are doing so at our own peril.

This experience has opened my eyes and brought to light one of life's most profound contradictions: We spend much of our time praying for peace while, to the contrary, we spend little or no time confronting our leaders who have perpetrated conflicts through the creation, dissemination, and use of weapons of war. If our prayers concerning peace are to be considered genuine, then let us ask ourselves, in what manner are we asking God to bring about peace? Would it be to remove all the weapons of war from the face of the earth? Or would it be to remove from the world those who are responsible for the creation, dissemination, and use of such weapons? In other words, what action or set of actions would we deem essential to influence our hearts and minds in such regard? It is in this context that we need to be reminded, "Surely God does not hear an empty cry, nor does the Almighty regard it" (Job 35:13, ESV). Also, let us "not be deceived: God is not mocked" (Galatians 6:7). Before we pray for peace, let us ask ourselves whether this is another

The Startling Revelation

ritual with no substance? Or are we genuinely asking God to follow through on our request, irrespective of the sacrifices required of us? Are we willing to do what is required of us to bring about peace?

To rid ourselves of destructive weapons, we need no supernatural intervention. We are the ones who have chosen this path just to satisfy our superficial egos and monetary interests. This is why, today, my plea is not directed at my former foster parents or deceased mass murderers. Instead, I am directing it at the living, whose actions are responsible for bringing about death and destruction to many, including innocent children.

In my reference to Hitler and the other mass murders, I am not equating or quantifying the results or the effects of their actions. Instead, I am highlighting our hearts' unwillingness to change, even when the evidence is overwhelming. My former foster parents must have known that their actions were causing grave harm to the children. Not to mention when they used those enhanced beating devices to physically abuse them and forced them to work in maggot-infested environments without the proper protective attire. As a result, the children had many open wounds and fungi that were rotting away their feet. Although the evidence was overwhelming, they would pretend not to notice or hear the children's cry. The only action they took was to ensure that the affected children were quarantined from the rest of the family. This unwillingness was also the same for those who ignored the behaviors of my former foster parents.

Therefore, let us examine the evidence before us and let the proof guide our actions. Once the truth has been uncovered, then let not the patriotism or allegiance we pledge to others or inanimate things sway our consciences to act otherwise. Patriotism and allegiance were the choices of many, including church members who knew that my foster parents were abusing the children but did nothing about it. As a result, their willingness to disavow the truth prolonged the abuse of the children.

My former foster parents heard the children's relentless cries for justice, which my brother expressed for over three and a half years. They heard the reasonable and persuasive arguments from total strangers, such as Mrs. Lee. I believe that they heard their consciences speaking to them concerning how they were treating the children. Nevertheless, they chose to ignore all three. I believe that God has given us the time and space to examine ourselves and change accordingly. I would hope that a third, a third, and a third would be sufficient warning for us to reverse the destructive course we are currently on.

ACCOUNTABILITY

Today, too many of us have adopted the "look the other way" attitude concerning injustice. This was the same mindset many had concerning my former foster parents, whose abusive behaviors were on full display. With this mindset, we have become unaware of our involvement and viewed those being harmed as merely "the Unknown," "the Distant Mother," "the Distant Father," and "the Distant Child." We are justifying our actions with false premises—"It is what it is," "This is the world we live in," "It is a fallen, broken world"—so there is nothing that we can do about injustice. This was the same mindset that many had concerning my former foster parents' "broken home." However, my brother did not see it that way. He tried desperately to transform

The Startling Revelation

the brokenness by confronting our foster parents, who were responsible. Unfortunately, he did not succeed in his endeavor. Instead, he was punished severely at the hands of those he had tried desperately to change.

I would hope that instead of referring to our current situation as a "fallen, broken world," we would realize that we have become "fallen, broken people" by allowing insanity to become the norm. It is within our power to make this world a better place. Therefore, it is irresponsible of us to think otherwise! Our unwillingness to accept responsibility is the fundamental reason why changing hearts and minds has been, and will always be, deemed "the Impossible."

Not only are we continuing to view our harmful actions as being justified, but we have erected thin veils and have drawn imaginary lines between our actions and the harm they cause to humanity. I believe this was the same concerning the leatherworker who was making and supplying my former foster parents with the devices they used to inflict much pain and suffering on the innocent children. I know this because the cries and the immense suffering borne by the innocent children have left me with a lifetime of emotional scars. In this context, I ask, who will be held accountable for the pain and suffering inflicted on the innocent children at the hands of my former foster parents? Is it only my foster parents, because of their direct involvement? Shouldn't the leatherworker also accept responsibility for being the maker and supplier of the devices used to harm the children? As a matter of fact, the children's physical and psychological suffering was intensified and prolonged the very day the leatherworker decided to supply my foster parents with those enhanced beating devices. I believe that the love of money caused

Chapter 1

the leatherworker to overlook the tangible evidence that was vividly on display. This is why I am calling on all, especially those in authority, not to sacrifice our human dignity in exchange for material or financial gain.

Many times, I found myself asking what my father meant when he claimed that the systems of this world should not be trusted and that those who profess Christianity are hypocrites. Why would my father do everything possible to shield his children from what society deemed the "acceptable norms"? I have often asked myself if there is a more equitable world out there for tomorrow's children. However, our actions' harmful results made me realize that instead of looking for an escape route out of this world, we can make it a better place by, first, accepting full responsibility and, second, relinquishing our harmful actions.

Seeing that my brother can no longer plead the cause for justice, I believe that the yearning cry that is needed to change hearts and minds must come from us. In this context, I would like to paraphrase the words that are inscribed on the outside rearview mirror of a motor vehicle: Although we are moving forward in time, we need to understand that the atrocities and aggressions of the past are "much closer than they appear." The only reason we can continue in such a manner is that our moral vision is grossly impaired. Although this analogy might not be apparent initially, I believe that if we pause for a moment and examine the consequences of our harmful actions, then and only then, might our minds be enlightened.

While living with my former foster parents, I chose to accept how we were treated as the norm. However, at no time did my brother accept such a premise. He tried desperately to change their hearts and minds, but to no

The Startling Revelation

avail. It is evident that the heart and mind of a reasonable person cannot be transferred to another. Each person's heart and mind must be willing to change based on the evidence being presented. I know that it is easy for us to look at my former foster parents and the others who have done grave injustice unto humanity and conclude that they were all evil. However, that is not the conclusion I would hope for us to derive from this experience. I hope that we could look deep within our souls and acknowledge that *we* are enablers and contributors to the systems and schemes that are continuing to bring about physical and psychological harm to humanity.

So, as people, systems, and nations, let us ask ourselves these fundamental questions: Am I willing to be held accountable for the transgressions for which I hold others accountable? Am I guilty of committing the very transgressions for which I am condemning others? Am I asking others to cease the actions that are deemed harmful to humanity while I am unwilling to do likewise? This is a reminder that we must hold ourselves and our leaders accountable because we are not immune to our actions' adverse effects.

I have outlined many flaws associated with my former foster parents and us and the need for us to change. So where do we begin? I believe a good starting point is here: "'And you shall love the Lord your God with all your heart and with all your soul and with all your mind and with all your strength.' The second is this: 'You shall love your neighbor as yourself.' There is no other commandment greater than these" (Mark 12:30–31, ESV). The above statement represents a sacred norm that society should embrace. This is an emotional plea for humanity as a whole, and one that reminds us that if we do

Chapter 1

not turn away from our harmful actions, then it will no longer be our past actions that haunt our souls, but those of the present. Also, "Behold, the fear of the Lord, that is wisdom, and to turn away from evil is understanding" (Job 28:28, ESV).

Although we cannot rewrite history, I believe that we have a moral obligation to write a better future, one in which we celebrate our differences and treat each other as human beings rather than enemies or adversaries. I have spent many years documenting my life experiences and throughout such time, I have searched diligently to see if there is any justification for my former foster parents' actions. However, the evidence has made it abundantly clear that there is absolutely no justification for their abusive behavior! Therefore, this is a desperate plea to everyone, but more so the younger generation. Please resist the urge to acquire riches at the expense of the less fortunate and the most vulnerable. Please let no one convince you that wars and the instruments of war are essential for your survival. The justifiable, necessary, and essential things are the noble acts of kindness and good deeds that are lacking throughout our society. Once again, this can only be possible if we heed the many calls (such as the ones outlined above) that are pleading to us to cease the actions that are harmful to humanity.

I hold myself accountable because when my brother spoke out against injustice, I told him to be quiet. When my brother reminded our foster mother that she should refrain from addressing us as dogs and scavengers, I said to him that being addressed as dogs and scavengers was a much lighter form of punishment than being physically abused. When my brother set conditions that we should not take care of the farm unless we were treated as human beings, I sided with my former foster parents against the plight of my own brother's cry for justice! I continued to take care of the farm, thus negating any possibility of our foster parents' acknowledging that their actions were wrong. I did so because I was afraid of being punished. I did so because I was concerned that we would lose the little provisions that they made available to us. However, I found out later that the very things I had tried so hard to protect, even at the expense of my only brother, lasted only for a short time. In this context, I hold myself accountable because I did not stand with my brother in his pursuit of justice. I have fallen short because I could only see the tangible things that benefited me. This is why I would like to say that it is time for all persons, systems, and nations to put justice above self-interest and so-called trustworthy alliances.

Therefore, whenever we can clearly see a person, system, or nation's deceitful actions on display, let us not associate ourselves with their actions simply because our interests are aligned with theirs. Let us not side with injustice because we have much to lose or gain from the outcome. The cost of forfeiting material possessions is a noble cause that should never be compromised by those who set out to destroy innocent lives in pursuit of ill-gotten gains.

Hearts and minds can be changed! I know that it is possible for us to cease the actions that are deemed harmful to humanity. This notion has proven to be true concerning my former foster parents. Throughout many of my conversations with Christopher (refer to volume 2 for context), he told me repeatedly that he had not received any of the abuse that the foster children were subjected to,

Chapter 1

which was quite difficult for me to believe at first. Nonetheless, to have learned that my former foster parents have changed has brought closure to a very painful chapter of my childhood. I hope someday Christopher could share his life story because his experiences contrasted those I outlined in my memoir.

Christopher was the only child who was born and raised in the care of my foster parents. Therefore, he had an opportunity to bond with them emotionally, which is something the foster children, and most likely, their adopted children, have not experienced. I wish all of us had the opportunity to talk with my foster parents and know when their hearts' conviction came about. This understanding would help us identify and address similar behaviors that are being perpetrated throughout the world.

Therefore, it is our responsibility to hold each other accountable in all situations, irrespective of our alliances and self-interests. I believe wholeheartedly that my foster parents could have made this change earlier had we stood up collectively and made it known that their actions toward the children were immoral. A collective voice of sanity should always preempt the unhinged forces of evil. The forces of good must be exercised at all times, especially in situations where injustice abounds. Finally, I would like to conclude by saying that we should not conform whenever we are faced with injustice but, instead, be transformed for the good of humanity.

CHAPTER 2

MY BELIEFS AND PHILOSOPHY

Now that you and I have learned much regarding me, my family, and the many wonderful, inspiring, and interesting people I have met along life's journey, I would like to share with you my philosophy as it relates to life. Before I proceed, I would like to ask two fundamental questions: What is life? And what constitutes life? According to the dictionary, and the many other scientific sources I consulted, life is the condition that distinguishes organisms from inorganic objects. However, as I delved into the other religious (Christianity as stipulated by the Bible) and philosophical sources, it has become quite clear that to define life using a single coherent term has posed challenges for scientists and philosophers alike. Irrespective of the many variations, I believe that life is really about living. With that said, I will try to answer these two fundamental questions based on the experiences that I have acquired as I have journeyed through life.

First, being able to compose my life's memoir has been a blessing for me. It made me realize that the fortunate and unfortunate situations that I have experienced did not happen to me by chance or mere coincidence. I believe that my experiences happened at specific times in my life to serve specific purposes. Therefore, the unfortunate circumstances surrounding my childhood have taught me the following:

- Being torn between ideologies and religious doctrines has helped me to identify with individuals who are caught up between the perceived norms and other religious and social ideologies of society.
- Being separated from my parents and placed in an orphanage and foster homes has helped me to understand and relate to the unfortunate children who have been abandoned or forcibly removed from their parents' care, with little or no regard for the physical and or psychological harm that is being done in the process.
- Having experienced extreme poverty, which included homelessness and hunger, has helped me to understand and sympathize with those who find themselves at the lowest tier of society.
- Having my hopes and dreams crushed by the very people who had promised to be my wonderful and loving foster parents has helped me to understand and to sympathize with others, especially innocent children whose hopes and dreams have been trampled on by those who have been entrusted to love and care for them.
- Having lost my only brother because he spoke out against injustice has helped me to understand and relate to any person, especially a child, who has been silenced and stripped of his or her dignity and

My Beliefs and Philosophy

God-given rights by those who seek to oppress and exploit the less fortunate.
- Finally, my life experience has allowed me to identify the correlation between our past actions and our actions today, and the need for us to renounce the actions deemed harmful to humanity.

Second, despite my unfortunate childhood circumstances, I realize that had it not been for those life experiences, I would not relate to the physical and psychological abuse that many children are going through. The adverse experiences have also taught me that I should not accept the notion that I am a victim of circumstances. Moreover, if I do, then that will be the day my life experiences cease to have meaning.

Third, to gain a better perspective of life, I have placed my faith in a higher being who is the creator and supreme ruler of the universe. Throughout my early childhood years, my father introduced me to Jah and told me that Jah is the creator and supreme ruler. However, throughout my later years, I was introduced to other labels, such as God and Jesus Christ. Nevertheless, this higher being remains true regardless of label, religion, denomination, creed, race, or gender. I also believe that all human beings are equal and that our actions are guided by our consciences. This precept also led me to believe that no other internal or external forces are more conclusive than our consciences. However, for us to take the actions that are in the best interests of humanity, our consciences should be guided and nurtured by good deeds.

Chapter 2

Fourth, after pondering the many experiences that have comprised my life, I have concluded that each person's attributes can be summed up with what I would describe as the **IDEA** factor. The IDEA factor represents a person's levels of **I**ndependence and **D**ependence, which are directly related to their levels of **E**ffort and **A**ffiliations. Throughout the childhood years, a person's level of dependence far outweighs the level of independence. However, a person's Effort and life's Affiliations will provide the means necessary to gradually build up the person's desired level of independence.

Fifth and final, I would like to use a relatable analogy to summarize my perspective as it relates to the IDEA factor of life. To highlight this point, I have used an illustration that depicts a group of kayakers being pushed downstream by a roaring river's unpredictable current. You can substitute my analogy with any other team-based activity to convey the same message.

Life is similar to a team of kayakers navigating the unpredictable current of a mighty river. Although the current is the dominant force that keeps the kayakers in motion, it is also important that they exercise caution due to its unpredictable nature. For their survival, these kayakers need to bond as a cohesive unit and be ready to provide a helping hand when called upon to do so. This illustration highlights the fact that although we are tightly bound to our individual lives, we do have unhindered abilities by which we can reach out to others whenever we are called upon to do so. The current and the movable and immovable obstacles symbolize life's natural forces, such as earthquakes, tornadoes, hurricanes, tsunami, typhoons, drought, and others, which we have limited control over.

My Beliefs and Philosophy

These are the forces by which we are swept up and carried along life's "mighty river." Nonetheless, we should strive to minimize the effects by taking heed of the evidence being presented and by using the limited resources at our disposal to attend to those affected.

I'm not skilled in philosophical discourse, and there are many intricacies to life's questions that I am still exploring. Nonetheless, my life experiences have taught me to hold dearly to three simple beliefs: First, I believe that life is a gift from God. Second, I believe that God's grace is always abounding. Third and final, I believe that God's love and forgiveness are unconditional. These beliefs provide me with a meaningful outlook on life. I am also encouraging you to reflect on some greater power (for me, that greater power is a Persona—God/Lord/Jah/Jehovah/Jesus Christ) to remind you that there is hope.

CONCLUSION

WHAT HAVE WE LEARNED?

While composing this memoir, I learned that even what we considered our most unpleasant life experiences do teach us things we would not have known otherwise. With that in mind, I composed A *Reflection of My Journey*, to summarize and share these life lessons, which is as follows:

- My life's experiences have opened my eyes to so much, and for that, I am grateful for the magnitude of God's grace and mercy bestowed unto me.
- My memoir has opened my eyes so that I could understand the true meaning of fostering.
- Having the opportunity to share my foster mother, Fredricka Lucy Brady (Aunt Lucy), with you has opened my understanding of her love and overwhelming compassion.
- I came one step closer to understanding my only brother's lifelong struggles and the fact that he did not receive the love and care he yearned for, but instead, was treated as an outcast.

Conclusion

- I realized that the family's strength and resilience are the two most essential characteristics that embody the pillars of our society.
- I realized that my life is the product of the many acts of kindness that others have bestowed unto me; these acts of kindness have made my life whole.
- I have learned that the decision to become a foster parent should be based *exclusively* on love and compassion and *not* as an avenue to fulfill one's selfish social or economic desires.

I hope that these life lessons remind us that life should not only be about "What is in it for me?" Instead, life can be more about, "What contributions can I make that will be of benefit to others, particularly the less fortunate children?"

Thank you for choosing to read my reflection, and may the divine principles of life guide you as you strive to make a positive impact on your life and the lives of others.

REFERENCES

Beyer, Catherine. "Introduction to the Beliefs and Practices of Rastafari." *Learn Religions*, www.learnreligions.com/rastafari-95695. Accessed 23 October 2020

"History of Rastafarianism." *ReligionFacts*, www.religionfacts.com/rastafarianism/history. Accessed 15 February 2017

"Rastafarianism." *History.com*, A&E Television Networks, www.history.com/topics/religion/history-of-rastafarianism. Accessed 31 May 2017

"Rastafarianism." *URI*, www.uri.org/kids/world-religions/rastafarianism. Accessed 23 October 2020

Reynolds, Ra Dennis Jabari. *Jabari Authentic Jamaican Dictionary of the Jamic Language: Featuring, Jamaican Patwa and Rasta Iyaric, Pronunciations and Definitions.* Around the Way Books, 2006.

Douglas, Frederick. *The Narrative of the Life of Frederick Douglass, an American Slave*, Published at the Antislavery Office, Boston, 1845. Chapter IX, pp. 53–54.

www.ingramcontent.com/pod-product-compliance
Lightning Source LLC
Chambersburg PA
CBHW021126080526
44587CB00010B/645